MICROSOFT POWERPOINT 2024

2024

A STEP-BY-STEP PRACTICAL GUIDE FOR BEGINNER AND ADVANCED USERS

CHARLES SHERER

TABLE OF CONTENT

INTRODUCTION

Microsoft PowerPoint 2024 is an up-to-date guide that provides you with everything you need to know about Microsoft PowerPoint. In this book, you will learn how to use the amazing features of PowerPoint, generate a professional PowerPoint presentation, and also make your slides act with each other by using animation and transition. This book will explain to you how to work with self-confidence and to be clever with MS PowerPoint tips, shortcut commands, and best practices. You will also learn how to insert and format pictures, shapes, charts, tables, and videos conveniently. Microsoft PowerPoint is not difficult to use, it is an easy-to-use software and effective tool for giving presentations. It has many amazing features for easy communication.

PowerPoint slides are admiringly modified to fit your contents, and needs, it has tools like SmartArt, tables, etc., to assist you in facilitating complex and multiple information into simple and easy-to-comprehend ones. It also assists in making your presentation enjoyable visually with features to include audio, pictures, video, animation, etc.

These tools will assist you to be more improvised and collaborative with the audience. PowerPoint permits you to work interactively with its review features, which permit notes and comments. You can distribute your PowerPoint presentation with your voice to anyone, everywhere, and even on Youtube unleashing any of its effects. PowerPoint has a lot of amazing features you might not be aware of if you did not learn the skill. When you learn the skill, it will make you work snappily, save time, and enhance your productivity.

CHAPTER ONE

The PowerPoint

To make usage of PowerPoint judiciously, this chapter reveals what constructing a PowerPoint presentation involves. As wonderful as PowerPoint can be, it also has its deprecators. It can come between the audience and the speaker if the software is not used in a manner marked by proper behavior. PowerPoint may be more of a thing that provides resistance, delay, or obstruction if the software is not used appropriately.

PowerPoint can now be found in almost every office around the world. It is unviable to sit in a seminar, or conference without sighting at least one PowerPoint presentation. I have heard of a nurse working in a hospital who makes the hospital known all over the world by way of a PowerPoint presentation at a conference. After a succinct journey with PowerPoint, you will have discovered how to create presentations, get an excellent view of your work, put together a photo album, insert slides, and hide slides.

Getting Familiarized with PowerPoint

The pictures below show the PowerPoint window. The slide which is the PowerPoint word for an image that you display to your spectators, is at the central of the window. There are a lot of tools that surround the slide for assigning decorating slides and text. On any or every occasion you want to display your slides to your spectators, you make use of the tools and cause the slide to appear on the screen, as displayed in the second picture below.

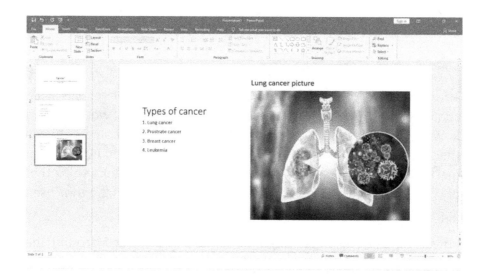

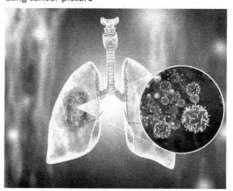

Lung cancer picture

Types of cancer
1. Lung cancer
2. Prostrate cancer
3. Breast cancer
4. Leukemia

Command to make PowerPoint, you have to be aware of a little terminology:

Note: This is the printed pages that the speaker, writes and prints so that he or she would be able to know what to say during the presentation, it is only the speaker that can see the notes. This will be explained in chapter 5 of this book.

Slides: The pictures you construct with PowerPoint. Slides come into sight onscreen one after the other, during a presentation.

Handout: This is a printed page that you may give to the spectators along with a presentation. It shows the slides in your presentation.

Presentation: Presentations are called slide shows. It comprises all the slides, from the beginning to the end, that you display to your spectators.

A Compressed Features Lesson

The picture below displays the various parts of the PowerPoint screen. This will help you to find your way around PowerPoint land, please note this aspect incase the screen terminology makes it more complex for you to comprehend any parts of the PowerPoint screen

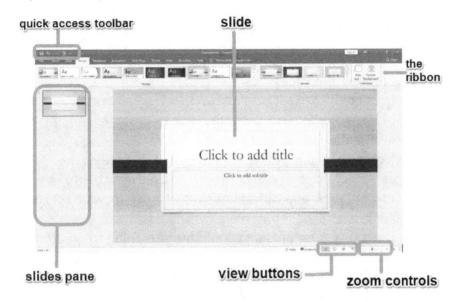

> ➤ **Quick Access toolbar:** You will notice this toolbar wherever you navigate in PowerPoint. It comprises- stare from beginning, undo, email, save, and repeat, you can also add as many features as you want.
> ➤ **The Ribbon:** This is a place where the tabs are positioned which comprises- File, Home, Insert, Design, Transitions, Slide Show, Animation, and so on.
> ➤ **Slide window:** This is where a slide or slides are displayed. When scrolling you will be able to navigate backward and forward in your presentation.

- ➢ **Slides pane:** This is located at the left-hand side of the screen, it is the area where you can see the slides or the text on the slides in your presentation.
- ➢ **View buttons:** These are the buttons you can click to switch to either left to right Normal, Reading View, Slide Sorter, and Slide Show.
- ➢ **Zoom controls:** These are the tools that are used for expanding or declining a slide (in Slide Sorter and Normal view).

A Windstorm Journey of PowerPoint

To help you apprehend what you are getting into, you are summoned on a windstorm journey of PowerPoint. Constructing a PowerPoint presentation demands accomplishing these essential tasks:

- ➢ **Creating the slides:** You can create the slides after you have created the newest presentation. PowerPoint provides a lot of preformatted slide designs, each designed to produce information in a definite way.
- ➢ **Notes:** You can put down notes in the notes pane, as you construct slides. Those notes can be used later to prepare your presentation and determine what to say to your spectators while each slide is onscreen.
- ➢ **Designing your presentation:** The next thing to do after you construct a presentation is to think about its appearance. You can reform slides' backgrounds and colors, you can also choose a theme for your presentation.
- ➢ **Inserting charts, tables, diagrams, and shapes:** Beginning on the insert tab, you can select charts, tables, diagrams, and shapes on slides as well as decorate your slides with text boxes, WordArt images, and shapes.

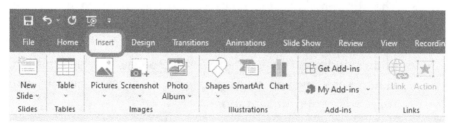

➤ **"Animating" your slides:** You can play sound and video via PowerPoint slides, as well as "Animated. You can cause the items on a slide to move on the screen.

➤ **presenting your presentation:** You can draw on the slides during a presentation, at the same time you can as well make the screen to be blanked and show slides out of order. You can also disburse presentations as videos, for instance, if you won't be there in person, PowerPoint gives you the advantage of creating self-running presentations and presentations that people can run personally.

Constructing a New Presentation

Each PowerPoint presentation is constructed using a template, A template is a layout for constructing slides. Each template comes with its specific slide layouts, fonts, and colors. If you have already opened a PowerPoint with a blank template, you can follow the steps below to see some other templates

1. click the file tab.

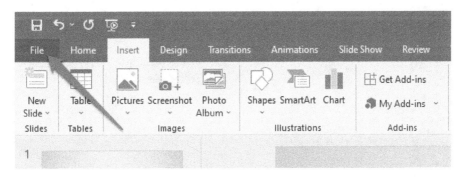

2. select 'New' from the left-hand side of the screen.

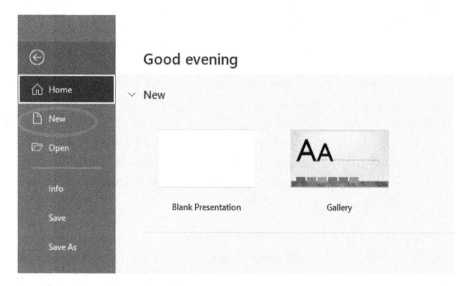

3. Then select a template from the many that appear.

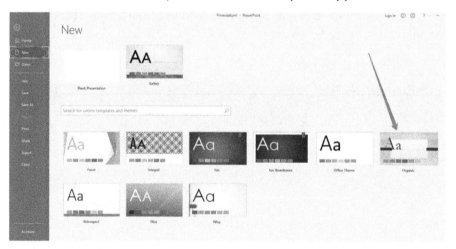

You may also be invited immediately after you create a presentation to select the template that is most appropriate for your audience.

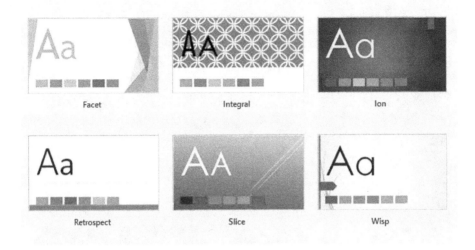

PowerPoint offers you different templates for constructing presentations:

- ➤ **Personal templates:** These are the kind of templates that you or someone else created that are different from that of the one Microsoft designed. A lot of businesses organization provides templates with their business colors and fonts for employees to make use of when creating PowerPoint presentations.

- ➤ **Office templates:** These are polished templates designed by Microsoft artists. The image below shows some of these templates in the New window, where you create presentations.

- ➤ **The Blank Presentation template:** This is a skeleton template that you can make use of as the beginning point for creating a presentation on your own.

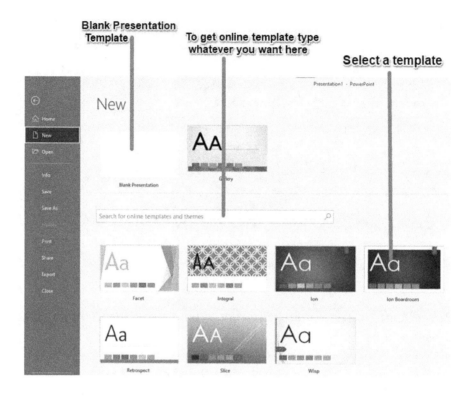

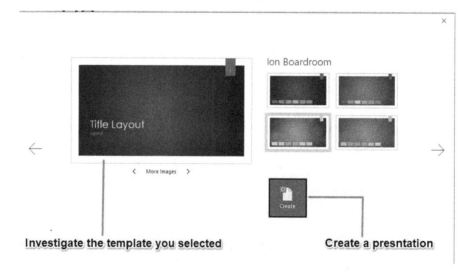

To create a PowerPoint presentation, follow the steps below:

1. Click the File tab.
2. Select New from the left side of the screen.

3. Then pick a template.

Select the template that is most appropriate for the spectators who will view your presentation.

- ❖ **Blank Presentation:** when you click the blank presentation icon, a new presentation is created.

Another way of creating a new blank presentation without even opening the New Window is by pressing Ctrl+N

- ❖ **Office template:** choose an Office template in the New Window. A model window opens so that you will be able to inspect carefully the slide layouts and themes that the template provides. You can search for a template by entering a search term in the search box. To return to the New windows, click on the close button, then click the create button to construct a presentation with the template you chose.
- ❖ **Personal template:** select the personal tab to go to the folder where you stored your templates. Then choose a template and click the create button. The personal tab comes into sight in the New window only if you have created one or copied it to your computer.

Guidance for Setting up Persuasive Presentations

Before you can build any slides, you have to think about what you want to disseminate to your spectators or audience. Your aim is not to greatly impress, charm, or beguile the audience with your PowerPoint, but to disseminate something, your aim and objective is to captivate the hearts of the spectators so that they would be able to apprehend the information you are passing to them. Below is some practical guidance for setting up a persuasive presentation:

❖ **Begin by writing the text in word:** It is advisable to start in Microsoft Word and not in PowerPoint so that you can concentrate on the words. In Microsoft word, you can undoubtedly see how a presentation emanates. You must make sure that your presentation establishes and develops to its rightful conclusion.

❖ **You need to consider the audience when choosing a design:** choosing a design determines the audience you are dealing with, a presentation to the champions of tomorrow deserves something splashy and bright while a presentation to the American Casket makers Association requires a quiet, mute design. Choose a slide design that sets the tone for your presentation and earns the compassion of the audience.

❖ **Follow the one-slide-per-minute rule:** At the very minimal, a slide should stay on the screen for at least one minute. Perhaps you have 20 minutes to talk, you are allowed no more than 20 slides for your presentation, according to the rule.

❖ **Keep it simple:** You need to keep it simple so that PowerPoint does not surpass you. Judiciously making use of the PowerPoint features, an animation in the right place at the right time can serve a high-value intention. It can honeypot an important aspect of a presentation and grasp the audience's attention. But filling a presentation with a lot of objects turns a presentation into a festival slideshow.

❖ **Beware of the bullet point:** There is a place for terse bullet points in a presentation, when you put them there, precisely to remind yourself of the next thing to say. Bullet points can cause tiredness. They can also be a diversion. When you are charmed to use a bulleted list, make sure you consider using a table, chart, or diagram instead.

❖ **Taking control from the beginning:** Make sure you spend the first minute introducing yourself to the spectators without operating the PowerPoint and make eye contact with the spectator. By doing this, you incorporate your acceptability. You give the spectators the chance to know who you are.

❖ **Make clear what you are about:** At the early stage, let what your presentation is all about be stated clearly, and what you contemplate to prove with your presentation. In other words, let your conclusion be stated at the start as well as the end. In this way, your spectators will be able to judge your presentation according to how well you construct your case, and they will be able to know what you are driving at.

❖ **Personify your presentation:** Make your presentation to be personalized. Tell your spectators your peculiar motive for being there or the reason why you are working for the company you represent. Knowing that you have a peculiar stake in the presentation, the spectators are more likely to belief you. They will understand that you are the speaker and not a spokesperson.

❖ **Telling a story:** People like listening to stories, everybody loves a relevant and well-delivered story. This piece of counsel is similar to the prior one about personifying your presentation. Naturally, a story establishes a problem for people and how to solve the problem.

❖ **Rehearse over and over again:** You will be less anxious when you have studied your material very well. If you don't want to be anxious make sure you rehearse your presentation over and over again until you know it backward and forward. Rehearse it as if you were in the presence of the spectators.

❖ **Use visuals and not only words:** To make your point don't use only words, apply visuals to your presentation, you are indebted to your audience for taking advantage of the pictures, diagrams, charts, and table efficiency of PowerPoint. People comprehend more pictures and words than they do understand from words alone. As the speaker, it is up to you, and not the slides, to discuss the topics in detail with words. Below are the data collections of some countries with their National Income(NI) represented in a table, and chart.

A Table

Country	National Income ($)
Canada	3.2million
USA	8.2million
Russia	7.3million
China	4.7million

A Chart

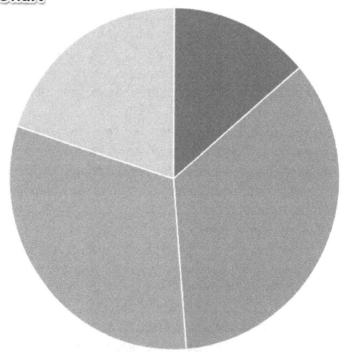

■ Canada ■ USA ■ Russia ■ China

CHAPTER TWO

Building New Slides for Your Presentation

Your next step on the footway to glory after you have created a presentation is to start adding up the slides. To build a slide, you begin by selecting a slide template. Slide templates are the preformatted slide designs that assist you impute text, graphics, and some other things. There are text placeholder frames for imputing titles and text in some slide templates while some are with content placeholder frames created most especially for imputing charts, diagrams, tables, images, pictures, or media clips.

When you insert a slide, choose the slide template that best almost accurately the slide you have had in mind for your presentation. The number 1-3 images below show the slide template that is accessible when you construct a presentation with the blank presentation template. These pages demonstrate how to impute slides and gather them from word document headings.

How to Insert a New Slide

Follow the steps bellow to insert a new slide in your presentation:

1. **Choose the slide that you want the new slide to follow.**
   Choose the slide on the slides pane, in normal view. Choose the slide in the main window, in the slide sorter view.
2. **On the insert tab or home, click on the bottom half of the New Slide button.**
   When you click on the top half of the New slide button, you will notice a drop-down list of slide layouts. Then choose a slide with the same layout you chose in step 1 above.

3. **Pick the slide template that best resembles the slide you want to construct.**
   you don't have to be worried about selecting the right layout. The slide layout can be changed later on by you.

Speediness methods for inserting slides

You can use these methods when you are in a hurry to insert a slide:

- ➤ **Building a duplicate slide:** choose the slide or slides you want to duplicate, from the insert or home tab, on the new slide button open the drop-down list and select duplicate selected slides.
- ➤ **Copying and pasting slides:** click the slide you want to duplicate, (to select more than a slide press the Ctrl key then click). Then click the copy button on the tab. Then click to choose the slide that you want the copied slide to appear after and click the paste button or press Ctrl+v.
- ➤ **Reclaiming or Recycling slide from other presentations:** choose the slide that you want the recycling slides to follow in your presentation, from the insert or home ribbon, open the drop-down menu on the New slide button, and select reuse slides. The reuse slides task pane will open up. Then click the Browse button, choose a presentation in the Browse dialog box, then click open. The reuse slides task pane displays thumbnail versions of the presentation you chose. Click slides to add them to your presentation, at once. To gather all the slides in the presentation, you can right-click a slide and select insert All.

Trickery slides from Word document headings

Word headings are the same as slide titles if you think about it very well. Headings, like slide titles, present a new topic. If you can navigate your way around the word and you want to get an upper start constructing a PowerPoint presentation, you can acquire the headings in a word document for your PowerPoint slides.

Immediately you import the headings from word, you obtain one slide for each Level 1 heading (headings stated the heading 1 style). Level 1 headings makeup the title of the slides, Level 2 headings makeup first-level bullets, Level 3 headings makeup second-level bullets, and so on. Paragraph text is not inserted.

Follow these steps to apply headings in a Word document to construct slides in a PowerPoint presentation:

1. **Click the outline view button from the View tab.** You will obtain a higher quality sense of how headings from the Word document land in your presentation by watching your presentation from the outline tab.

2. **Choose the slide that the recent or new slides from the Word document will follow.**
3. **On the insert or home tab, open the drop-down list on the recent slide button and select slides from the outline.**

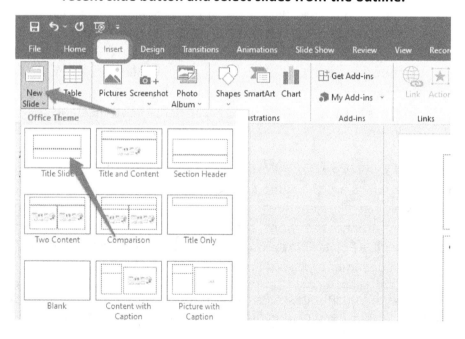

4. **Choose the Word document with the headings you want for your presentation and click on the insert button.**

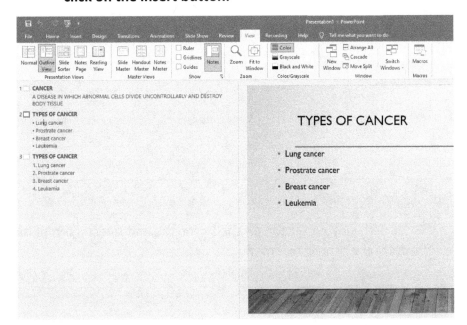

Choosing a distinctive template for a slide

If you choose the wrong template for a slide mistakenly, that is not the end you can start all over again. By using one of these methods you can insert a new template upon your slide:

❖ Right-click the slide (you must be very careful not to right-click an object or a frame), select the layout, and choose a template on the drop-down list.

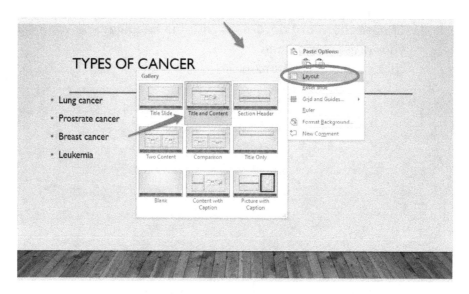

❖ Click the layout button on the Home tab and select a template from the drop-down menu.

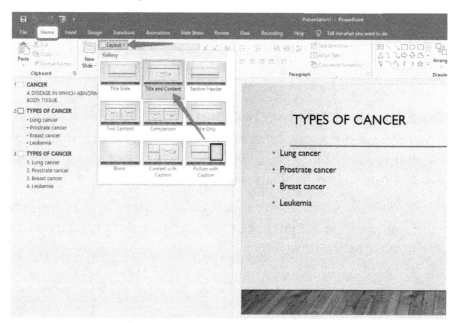

Obtaining a Better View of Your Work

Certain views are better than others, contingent on the work at hand. In this aspect, I will be explaining how to change views and the dependent features of Normal, Notes page, Slider sorter, Reading View, Slide Master, Handout Master, and Notes Master view.

Changing views

There are two ways of changing the view in PowerPoint:

➢ **View tab:** On the View tab, click a button in the Master Views group or presentation Views.

➢ **View buttons on the status bar:** Click a View Button-Slide Sorter, Normal, Slide Show, or Reading view- on the status bar to change view. See the image below:

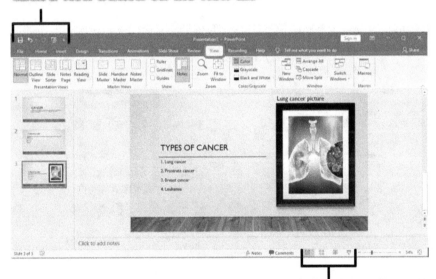

click a view button on the view tab

or click a view button on the status bar

Looking at the diverse views

See the appraisal of the diverse views with an idea about using each one below:

❖ **Normal view for inspecting slides:** Change to Normal view and choose a slide in the slides pane when you want to inspect a slide. In Normal view, brief slides come into sight in the slides pane, and you can view your slide at the central of the screen.

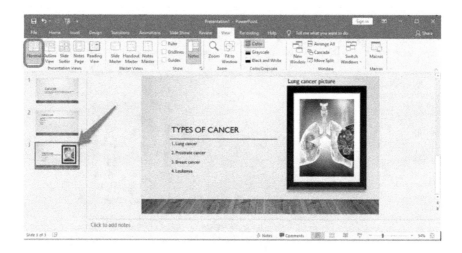

❖ **Outline view for piddling with text:** Change to outline view whenever you what to read or impute text. Outline view is perfect for editing text in a presentation, immediately you click

Outline view you will notice that the words appear in outline form on the left side of the screen.

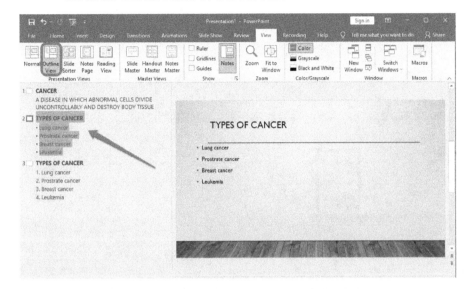

❖ **Slide sorter view for deleting and moving slides:** In the slide sorter view, you will see frames of all the slides in the presentation (make use of the zoom slider to change the size of frames). The slides are numbered for you to view where they appear in a presentation. Moving slides around is simple and viewing a lot of slides synchronically gives you a faculty of whether the diverse slides are consistent with one another and how the whole presentation is fashioning up.

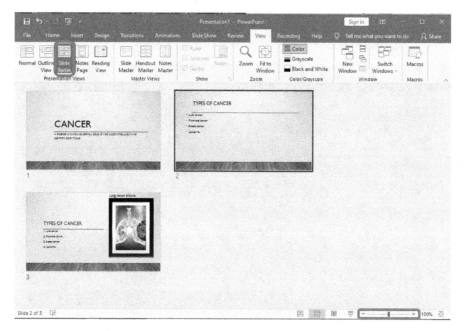

❖ **Note page view for reading your speaker notes:** Note page view permits you to see notes you've written to help you in your presentation, in case you have written any.

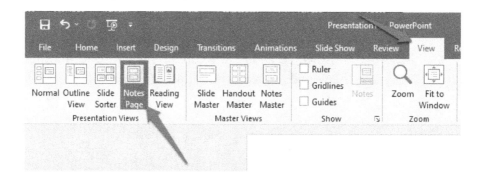

❖ **Reading view for focusing on slides' materialization:** Reading view allows you to see a single slide, but it will show on the screen with the view buttons, and also with the moving button to move faster from slide to slide. Change to Reading view for slides proofreading and do the final brushes on a presentation.

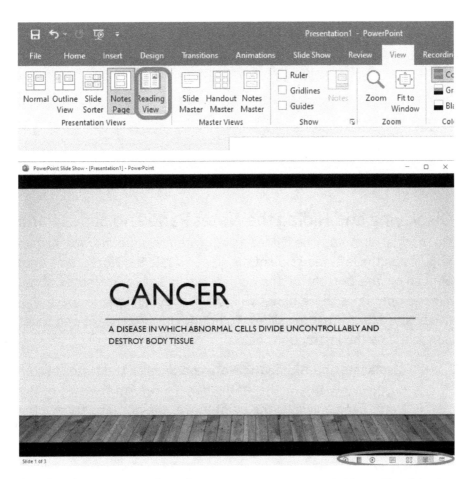

❖ **The Master view for a constant presentation:** The Master view comprises Slide Master, Handout Master, and Notes Master, they are for running master styles, arranging commands that concern all the slides in a presentation, notes, and handouts. To change to these views proceed to the View tab and click the proper button. Master styles and master slides will be explained in chapter 2 of this book.

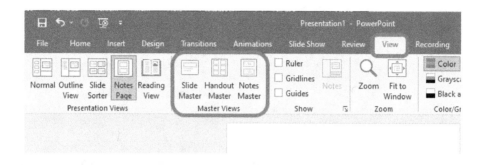

Displaying and Hiding the Notes Pane and Slides Pane

On normal ground, The Slides pane with its slide frames always appears on the left-hand side of the screen while the Notes pane does appear on the bottom of the screen for you to write notes about slides. Sometimes these panes will just occupy high-value space that can be used for formatting slides. To briefly close the Notes and Slides panes, follow the instructions below:

- ❖ **Displaying and Hiding the Notes pane:** click the Notes button on the View tab or the status bar. To reform the size of the Notes pane, navigate the pointer over the border between the pane and the rest of the screen, you can now drag the border immediately after the pointer changes to a double-headed arrow.
- ❖ **Displaying and Hiding the slides pane:** To hide the Slides pane, shift the pointer over the border within the pane and the central of the screen, and drag the border to the left when the pointer reforms to a double-headed arrow. Click the frames button to show the slides pane (positioned at the top of the slides pane).

Choosing, Moving, and Deleting Slides

In the presentation, you have to shift slides forward and backward. Occasionally you have to delete a slide. And you can't delete or move slides until they are selected. Below are the guidelines for selecting or choosing, moving, and deleting slides.

Choosing slides

The best place to choose slides is the Slide Sorter view. Use one of these methods to choose slides:

- ➤ **Choose a single slide:** click the slide.
- ➤ **Choose various diverse slides:** hold down the Ctrl key then click the slide in the slide sorter view or the slide pane.
- ➤ **Selecting all the slides:** click the select button on the Home tab then choose Select All from the drop-down list.
- ➤ **Choose a block of slide:** from the slide sorter view, drag over the slides you want to choose. make sure when you click and begin to drag that you do not click a slide.
- ➤ **Choosing various slides in succession:** hold down the shift key and click the first slide and then the last slide.

Moving slides

To move slides, it is thoughtful for you to go to Slide Sorter view. Choose the slide or slides that you want to move and apply one of these methods to move slides:

- ➤ **Cutting and pasting:** cut the slide or slides on the Home tab to the Windows Clipboard (click the Cut button, and press Ctrl+X). Then choose the slide that you want the slides to appear after and give the paste order (right-click and select paste or click the paste button then press Ctrl+V)
- ➤ **Dragging and dropping:** click the slides you had chosen and drag them into a new place.

Deleting slides

Think very well before you delete a slide. Choose the slide or slides you want to delete and apply one of these methods to erase or delete them:

- ➤ Right-click and select the delete slide on the shortcut menu
- ➤ Press the delete key.

Placing Together a Photo Album

The photo album is just PowerPoint's terminology for imputing a lot of photographs into a presentation at once. You don't need fully have to package the photo album with baby pictures for it to be an appropriate photo album. The Photo Album is an amazing feature because it can be used to dump a bunch of photos in a PowerPoint presentation without creating slides at once, impute the photo, and undergo the long and complicated procedure that seems tiresome. Create a photo album to quickly plot a bunch of photos on PowerPoint.

Creating your photo album

A new presentation will be created for you by PowerPoint when you create a photo album. To commence, make sure you know where you can locate the photo you want to use on your computer. Then go to the Insert tab and select the photo album button. You will see the photo album dialog box as displayed in the second image below. For such a small thing, the photo album dialog box provides a lot of privileges for building a PowerPoint presentation. Your first work is to make a decision on which pictures you want for your album. Then you select a slide template for the pictures.

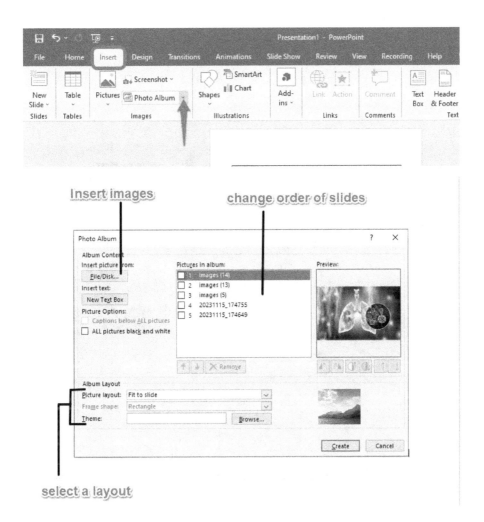

Inserting pictures and creating slides

Here is the information on selecting pictures for a photo album:

> **Inserting photos:** click the File/Disk button, choose images in the insert New Pictures dialog box, then click the insert button. You can choose beyond one photo at a time by pressing down the Ctrl key and then clicking the photos. The filenames of the selected photos are displayed in the pictures in the Album box,

the slide numbers will also appear for you to know which photos are on which slides.

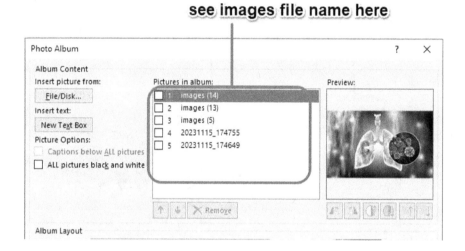

> **Deciding how photos are framed:** click the Frame shape and select an option from the drop-down menu for placing rounded corners or borders on your pictures. The options will not be available if you select fit to slide on the picture layout drop-down menu.

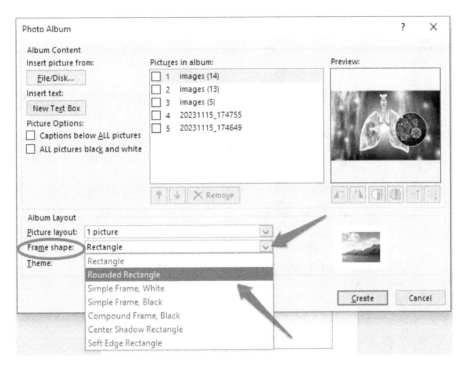

➢ **Inserting a text box:** if you want to enter an article or piece written you will need to insert a text box. In the pictures in the album box, choose the text box or pictures that you want your resent text to follow; then click the new text box button. Then you can now later go into your presentation and edit the placeholder text, which PowerPoint appropriately enters as Text Box.

➢ **Changing the order of pictures:** choose a picture in the pictures in Album box and then click the arrow button to shift it backward or forward in the presentation.

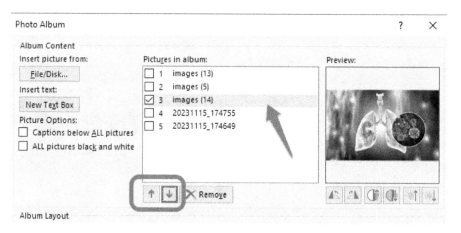

> ➢ **Removing a picture:** choose a picture in the pictures in the Album box and click the remove button to delete it from your photo Album.

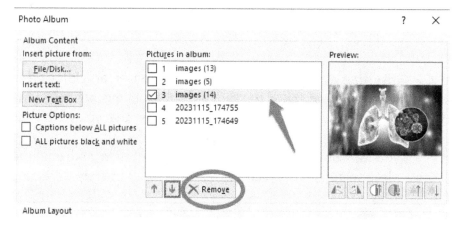

> ➢ **Changing the order of slides:** hold down the Ctrl key then begin to choose each picture on a slide. Then click an arrow as many times as you wish to shift the slide forward or backward.
>
> ➢ **Provision of captions for all pictures:** To provide a caption beneath all the pictures in your photo Album, choose the Caption Beneath All Pictures check box. PowerPoint originally positions the picture filename in the caption, but you can cancel the caption and then impute your own. To choose this caption, you must select a picture layout option nearby Fit to Slide.

Selecting a layout for slides

The next thing you need to do is visit the lowest part of the photo album dialog box and select a template or layout for the slides in the presentation. Open the picture layout drop-down list to select one of the picture layouts:

- Select Fit to slide for a presentation in which each picture engages a whole slide.
- Select a 'pictures' option to fit 1 or 2 pictures on each slide.
- Select a 'picture with' option to fit 1, or 2 pictures as well as a text title frame on each slide.

Reshaping the look of pictures

The Photo Album dialog box provides a lot of tools for changing or reshaping the look of the pictures. When looking at these tools, make sure you gaze your eye on the Preview box- it displays to you what you are doing to your pictures.

- **Making all photos black and white:** Choose the All Pictures Black and White check box
- **Changing the contrast:** select a contrast button as many times to mute or sharpen the light and dark shades or colors in the picture.
- **Rotating pictures:** click the Rotate button to rotate clockwise or anticlockwise.
- **Changing the brightness:** click the Brightness Button as many times as possible to make the image brighter or less bright.
- **Picking a theme for your photo album:** If you chose a 'picture" or "picture with" slide layout, you can select a theme for your slide presentation. Click the Browse button and select a theme in the choose dialog box.
- **Selecting a frame shape for pictures:** if you desire a "picture" or "picture with" slide layout, you can select a shape-compound, frame, Soft Edge Rectangle, or others- for your on the Frame Shape drop-down menu.

Finally, click the create button when you are set to create the photo album. PowerPoint gives a title slide at the beginning of the album that says Photo Album with your name beneath.

Laying on the final touches

Depending on the options you selected for your photo album, it requires all or a few of these final touches:

- ➢ **Write the captions:** if you requested photo captions, PowerPoint inserted photo filenames beneath photos. Change these filenames with something more explanatory.
- ➢ **Fill in the text boxes:** if you requested text boxes with your photo album, make sure you change the PowerPoint overall text with significant words generated by you
- ➢ **Fix the title slide:** The title slides you chose should speak more than the words Photo Album and your name.

Editing a photo album

Returning to the Photo Album dialog box and reorganize the photos in your album, go to the insert tab, open the drop-down catalog on the Photo Album button, and select Edit Photo Album on the drop-down catalog. You view the Edit Photo Album dialog box. It works and looks perfectly like the Photo Album dialog box. Yes, you can edit your photo album by handling it like any other PowerPoint presentation. Reform the theme, dabble with the slides, and do what you will to turn your photo album into shape.

Hidden Slides for All Contingencies

If you want to keep a slide on hand you can hide it "just in case" during a presentation. Slides that are hidden do not appear in slide shows except if you bring them out of hiding. The presenter can view the hidden slides in Slide Sorter view and Normal view, the spectator won't be privileged to view them while the presentation is going on unless you show them. You can buttress your point by showing your spectators the hidden slide in the course of the presentation.

Hiding a slide

The appropriate place to insert hidden slides is at the end of the furthermost part of a presentation, where you know they can easily be found. Follow the steps below to hide slides:

➤ **Choose the slide or slides you want to hide**
➤ **Click the Hide Slide button, On the Slide Show tab.**

you can also right-click a slide in the slide sorter view or slide pane and select Hide Slide. Then in the slide sorter window or slide pane, the Hidden slides' numbers are crossed through. Click the Hide Slide button once again or right-click the slide and select Hide Slide to unhide a slide.

Displaying a hidden slide during a presentation

During the progress of the presentation, hidden slides won't show up, but you can show them if the need arises. To display a hidden slide during the presentation, follow these steps bellow:

➤ **Click the slides button positioned at the lower-part corner of the screen.**
You will notice a screen with brief versions of slides in your presentation, you can as well open this screen by right-clicking and selecting See All Slides.
➤ **Choose a hidden slide so that the spectators can see it.**
You can tell which slides are hidden because their slide numbers are encased in brackets.

How do you go back to your presentation after seeing a hidden slide? If you are looking at only one hidden slide, you can right-click and select last viewed on the shortcut menu to go back to the slide you saw before the hidden slide. In case you have viewed many hidden slides, right-click the screen, select See All Slide, and choose a slide to resume where you left off.

CHAPTER THREE

Customizing a Look for Your Presentation

From the spectator's point of view, this chapter is the most relevant in this book. What your presentation looks like-which the theme and background style you choose for the slides in your presentation-lays the tone. From the first slide, the spectator will judge your presentation on its occurrence. When you fashion a look for your presentation, you are affirming what you want to disseminate to your spectators. This chapter describes how to deal with backgrounds. It inspects what you need to contemplate when you choose designs and colors for backgrounds. You will also learn how to choose and modify a theme, and how to create your slide backgrounds. This same chapter also looks into how to reform the background of some but not every slide in a presentation. It also teaches how to use master style and master slide to make sure that slides are consistent with one another throughout your presentation.

Viewing Themes and Slide Backgrounds

The theme you selected and the slide backgrounds you create for the slides in your presentation, mostly determine what a presentation looks like. A theme is a "bottled" slide design. Themes are fashioned by graphic artists. Many themes include complex background patterns and colors. You can also create a personal background from a single color, a gradient mixture of two colors, or a picture.

The image below displays examples of themes. When you install PowerPoint on your computer, you also install a lot of themes, and you can get more themes on the internet. Immediately after you choose a theme, you can choose a theme variant-a slight difference from the theme you chose.

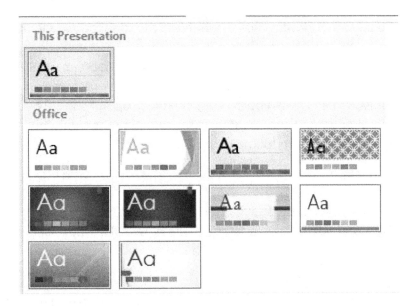

To select a theme or create slide backgrounds, begin on the design tab, as shown in the image below. The design tab provides theme variants, themes, and the format Background pane, which you visit when you want to design a designable background for slides.

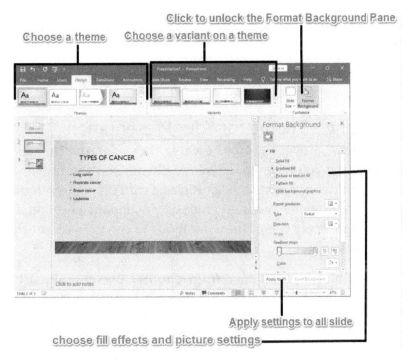

Beyond any other design choice, what lays the tone for a presentation are the colors you choose for slide backgrounds. You can choose hot colors or light-tone for the slide if your presentation aims to display photographs you took on a holiday. But if your presentation is an antagonistic sales angle, you can select a black background. There are no general or compulsory principles for selecting the right colors in a design you just need to follow your perception.

OBTAINING DESIGN IDEALS FROM POWERPOINT

PowerPoint may assist you with designing examples for a slide in your presentation. Follow these steps bellow to take your clue from PowerPoint and change the view of a slide:

- ➢ choose the slide
- ➢ On the design tab or Home tab, choose the designs ideas button.

  Incase PowerPoint will be helpful, slide designs will come into sight in the design ideas tab.

- ➢ Choose a design to implement to the slide you chose.

  You can click the undo button incase the design does not captivate enough for you.

Selecting a Theme for Your Presentation

PowerPoint provides various diverse themes in the themes gallery, and in case you have PowerPoint at hand, you can obtain a theme from another presentation. Scrutinizing with themes is not difficult. It is good to examine diverse themes till you find the best one. From the design tab, apply one of these methods to choose a resent theme for your presentation:

- ➢ **Obtaining a theme from another presentation:** select the design tab, open the Themes gallery, and click browse for Themes. From the dialog box that appears you will see choose Theme or Theme Document. find and choose a presentation with a theme appropriate for your presentation then click the apply button.

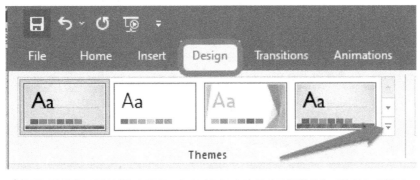

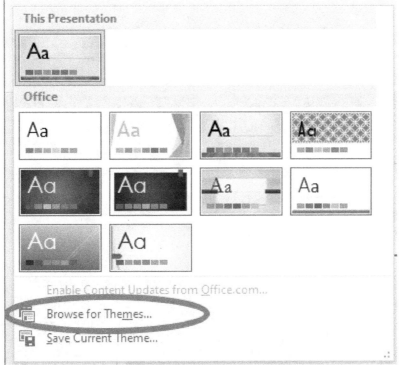

➤ **Choosing a theme in the themes gallery:** Open the Themes gallery and shift the pointer above diverse themes to "live-preview" them. Then click a theme to choose it.

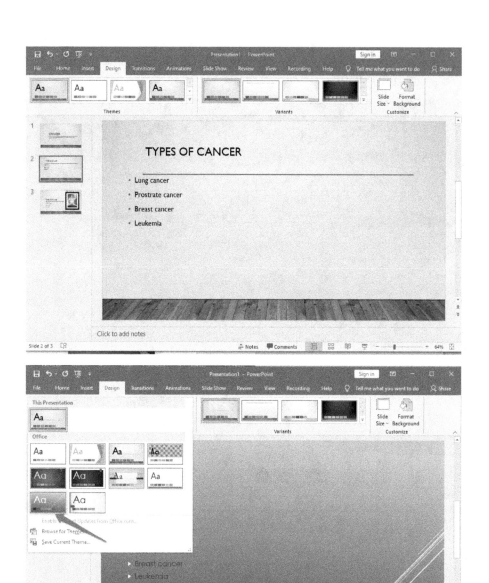

Building slide background on your own

Beyond a theme, another option you have for building or creating slide backgrounds is to do it personally. For the background, you can have a gradient blend of colors, transparent color, solid color, an image, or a picture.

- ❖ **Gradient:** A mixture of diverse colors with the colors mixing into one another.
- ❖ **Solid color:** A distinct color. You can modify a color's transparency and in effect "bleach out" the color to drive it farther into the background.
- ❖ **Texture:** A steady pattern that provides an impact that the slide is shown on a material such as stone or cloth.
- ❖ **Pattern:** A pattern such as diamonds or stripes.
- ❖ **Picture:** A picture you derived from the store on your computer or the internet.

Using a transparent or solid color for the slide background

When you use a transparent or solid color for the background it will give your slides a sincere or honest appearance. Follow these steps bellow to apply a transparent or solid color as the background for slides:

- ❖ **Select the design tab, then select the format background button.**

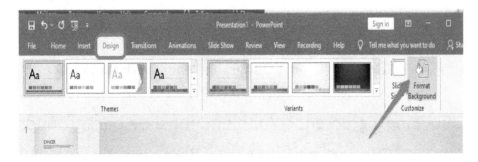

The Format Background pane opens to see the image bellow:

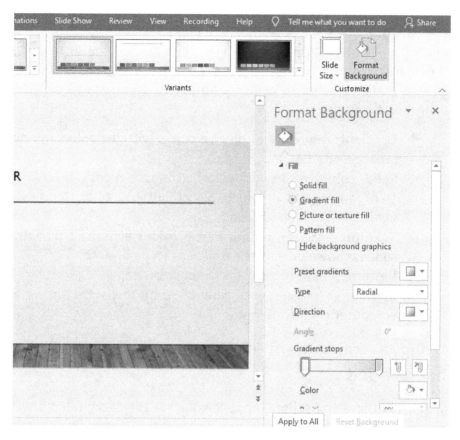

You can also scroll downward to view more options or details about the Format Background.

❖ **Click the solid fill options button.**
❖ **Click the color button and choose a color on the drop-down menu.**
❖ **If you want a "bleached out" color rather than a slide color, Drag the Transparency slider.**
❖ **To close the Format Background pane, click the Apply to All button and then the close button.**

Building a gradient color blend for slide backgrounds

Gradient simply means how and where two or more colors blend or grade, into one another on a slide. You can choose a rectangular, radial, or path gradient direction, using a gradient is an exceptional path to create an original background that is not the same as the other presenter's slide backgrounds.

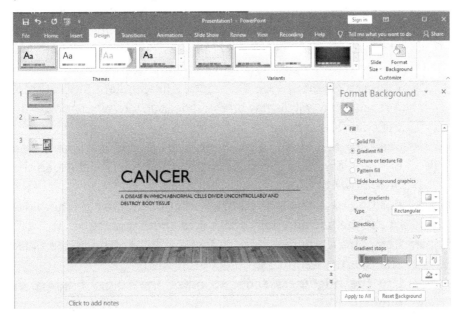

This is an example of a gradient fill slide as you can see I choose Rectangular as the type, and you can select Radial, Path, or Shade as the type.

Follow the steps bellow to create a gradient background for the slide:

1. **Select the design tab, then open the Format Background pane.**
2. **Click the Gradient fill options button:** Before you evaluate with gradient, try to open the preset Gradients drop-down list to view whether one of the ready-made gradients has done the job for you.

3. **On the type drop-down menu, select what type of gradient you want- Radial, Rectangle, Path, or linear from the title see the image above, and I pick Rectangular.**

    You can modify the angles at which color bends in case you select linear

47

4. **Create a gradient stop for each color transition you want on your slides:** Gradient stops decide where colors are, how colors transition from one to the other, and which colors are used. You can create a lot of gradient stops as you want. Below are methods for dealing with gradient stops:

➢ **Adding a gradient stop:** Select the Add Gradient Stop button. A resent stop will display on the slide. pull it to where you want the color blend to be

➢ **Selecting a color for a gradient stop:** choose a gradient stop on the slider, click the color button then select a color on the drop-down catalog.

➢ **Positioning a gradient stop:** pull a gradient stop on the slider or use the position box to shift it to another place.

➢ **Removing a gradient stop:** choose a gradient stop on the slider and click the Remove Gradient Stop button.

➢ **Use the brightness slider to make the colors brighter or dimmer.**

➢ **Use the Transparency slider to make the colors on the slides less or more transparent.** you will have solid colors at 0% transparency but at 100% you will have no color at all.

➢ **Click the Apply to all button.**

Putting a picture in the slide background

Office.com provides countless photos and pictures. You will be invited to put one in the background of your slides by following the steps below:

➢ **Click the design tab, then select the format Background button.**

➢ **Select the Picture or Textile fill button.**

➢ **Then click the insert button.** You will notice the insert Picture dialog box.

➢ **Search and choose a picture that you use in the background of your slides.**

➢ **Enter a transparency measurement in the background pane.** Enter a measurement in the box or pull the transparency slider. The greater the measurement, the more transparency, see the image below.

➢ **To make your picture fill the slide, enter measurements in the Offsets boxes.**

➢ **Select the Apply to All button and then click the Close button in the Format Background Pane.**

The picture you chose will appear immediately in the slides' backgrounds.

Using your personal photo for a slide background

If you don't want to use images or photos from the internet, you can use your personal photo. The photo below is a sample of personal images used as slide backgrounds, apart from the one gotten from the internet.

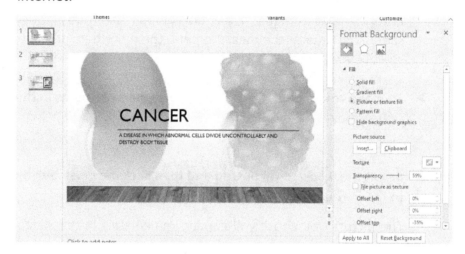

Follow the steps below to use your picture as a slide background:

1. **Click the Design tab, then select the Format Background button to open the Format Background pane.**
2. **Click the Texture or Picture Fill option button.**
3. **Click the insert button.**
   A drop-down catalog asks where to get the image.
4. **Click the From a File button.**
   The insert picture dialog box displays.
5. **Search for the photo you want, choose it, and then click the insert button.**
   The picture will appear on your slide immediately.
6. **Apply the transparency button to make the picture fade a little bit.**
7. **Make use of the Offsets text boxes, and impute measurements to make the image fit on the slides.**
8. **Select the Picture icon in the Background pane.**

9. **To make your image more fitted for a background, investigate the Picture corrections and Picture color options.**
10. **Then click the Apply to All button.**

Applying a texture for a slide background

Using texture is another option for slide backgrounds, a texture provides the impact that the slide is shown on a material such as parchment or marble. Kindly follow these steps to apply a texture as a slide background.

1. **Select the Design tab, then click on the Format Background button to unlock the Format Background pane.**
2. **Select the Picture or Texture Fill option button.**
3. **Click the Texture button and select a texture on the drop-down catalog.**
4. **Drag the transparency slider or Impute a transparency measurement to make the texture less grand and impressive in appearance.**
5. **Select the Apply to All button and then click close.**

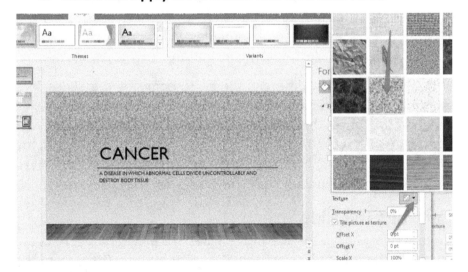

I selected brown marble from the Texture drop-down catalog, we have Canvas, Papyrus, and so on, you can choose any texture you like from the Texture drop-down catalog.

Modifying the Background of a Single or Handful of Slides

If you want to make a single or handful of slides to be easily noticeable in a presentation, modify or change their theme or background. A distinct or different background shows your audience that the slide being presented is somehow different from the one before it. Apply a distinct background or theme to make a transition, showing that your presentation has changed gears.

Follow these steps to modify the background of a single or several slides in your presentation:

1. **Select the Slide Sorter view from the View tab, then pick the slide or slides that require a different look.**
   You can choose more than one slide by Ctrl+clicking slides

2. **On the Design tab, select a different background or theme for the slides you chose.**
   How you apply this depends upon whether you are working with a slide background or a theme:
   - **Slide background:** Do it as if you are creating a background style for all the slides, but do not click on the Apply to All button
   - **Theme:** From the Themes gallery, right-click a theme and select Apply to All button

When you appoint a different theme to some of the slides in a presentation, PowerPoint produces another Slide Master. You may be amazed to notice that when you impute a new slide to your presentation, a second, or third set of slide templates displays on the New Slide drop-down catalog. These extra templates are displayed because your presentation has more than a single Slide Master.

Selecting the Slide Size

To modify or change the size of the slides in a presentation, navigate to the Design tab and select the Slide Size button. Then, from the drop-down catalog, select Standard (4:3), select Widescreen (16:9), or select Custom Slide Size and select a distinct size in the Slide Size dialog box. Note that All slides in a presentation must be equal in size. For your information, you can't combine and matchup different sizes.

Employing Master Slides and Master Styles for a constant Design

Constancy is everything in a PowerPoint design. The constancy of design is a sign of care and professionalism. In the interest of constancy, PowerPoint provides master slides and master styles. Commencing from a master slide, you can modify or change a master style and, in the process, reformat a lot of slides the same way. These pages clarify how master slides can speedily assist you in redesigning a presentation.

Swapping to Slide Master view

To use master slides, swap to slide Master view, as shown in the image below. From this view you can begin to work with master slides:

1. **click the View tab.**
2. **Select the Slide Master button.**
   You can choose a master slide in the Slides pane, in Slide Master view, format styles on a master slide, and in the same manner reformat various diverse slides. (click the Close Master View button or a view button such as Slide or Normal Sorter to leave Slide Master view).

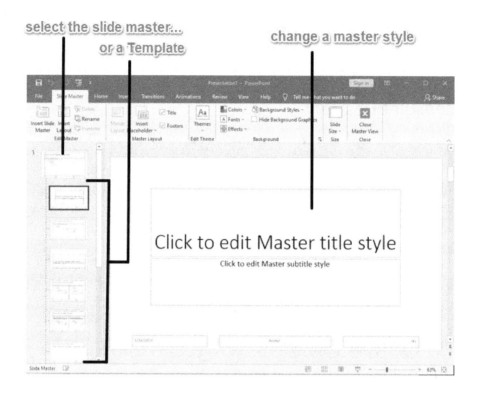

Understanding master slides and master styles

- ➤ **The Slide Master:** This is the first slide in the Slides pane in the Slide Master view. It is a little bit larger than the Master Slides. The formatting changes you make to the Slide Master will influence all the slides in your presentation.

- ➤ **Layout:** In Slide Master view, PowerPoint gives one layout for each type of slide layout in your presentation. By choosing and reformatting a layout in Slide Master view, you can redesign all slides in your presentation that were created with the same slide layout. For instance, to change or modify alignments, fonts, and other Formats on all the slides that you constructed with the Title layout, Choose the Title layout in Slide Master view and modify or change master styles on the Title layout.

- ➤ **Master styles:** Every master slide- the Slide Master and every layout- provides you the privilege to click to edit master styles.

The master style controls how text is formatted on slides. By reforming a master style on a master slide, you can modify the appearance of slides across a presentation. For instance, by changing or modifying the Master Title Style font, you can reform fonts in all the slide titles in your presentation.

Editing a master slide

To edit a master slide, go to slide Master view, choose a master slide, and change or reform a master style. To impute a picture on a master slide, select the insert tab.

Changing or modifying a master slide layout

Changing the layout of a master slide requires changing the size and position of text frames and content frames and also eliminating these frames:

➢ **Changing the size of frames:** choose the frame you want to modify, and then shift the pointer over a frame handle on the corner, side, above, or beneath the frame and drag when you notice the double-headed arrow.
➢ **Moving frames:** Shift the pointer over the border of a frame, click when you notice the four-headed arrow, and drag.
➢ **Adding a frame to the slide Master:** choose the slide master, and on the slide master tab, select the Master Layout button. You notice the Master Layout dialog box. Choose the check box beside the name of every frame you want to include then click OK.

CHAPTER FOUR

Inserting the Text

In this chapter I will be explaining how to change or reform the appearance of text, creating text boxes, and text box shapes. I unravel the puzzle of what to do when the text doesn't fit in a text box. You will also know how to align text, deal with numbered and bulleted lists, and include footers and headers on all or some of the slides in your presentation.

Inserting Text

The first thing you notice when you add a new slide to a presentation are the words "Click to add text." Immediately you click, the words of instruction will dematerialize, and you will have access to insert a title or text of your own. The simplest way to insert text on slides is to click in the text placeholder frame and start typing. The other means is to go to Outline view and insert text in the Slides pane.

Insert text on slides in the same manner you insert text in a Word document. in the process you can change fonts, the font size of the text, and also the color of the text.

Selecting fonts for text

In case you are not satisfied with the fonts in your presentation, there are two ways to solve the problem:

> **Delve in and select new fonts on a slide-by-slide basis:** choose the text, move to the Home tab, and pick a font drop-down catalog. You can also modify or change fonts in the mini-toolbar that come into sight immediately after you choose text.

> **Pick a new font on a master slide to change fonts across your presentation:** Master slides have been explained in chapter two of this book, and how to apply them to change formats

concurrently on a lot of slides. In slide Master view, choose a master slide and modify its fonts on the home tab.

Changing the font size of the text

Move to the Home tab and choose the text whose size you want to modify or change. Then apply one of these techniques below to modify font sizes:

➢ **Font dialog box:** pick the font group button to open the font dialog box. Then either enter a point size in the size text box or select a point size from the size drop-down list and click OK.

➢ **Increase Font Size and decrease Font Size buttons:** To increase or decrease the point size by the next interval on the Font Size drop-down catalog, press Ctrl+Shift> orCtrl+Shift<. Observe the font size list or your text and see how the text changes size.

➢ **Font Size drop-down catalog:** Open this list and select a point size. To select a point size that is not on the list, pick the Font Size text box, input a point size, and press Enter. You can also change or modify font sizes in the mini-toolbar that comes into sight immediately after you choose text.

Changing the look of the text

PowerPoint provides about a hundred diverse ways to change the look of text. You can make the text glow, change the colors, and make the text launch a shadow, among other things. Apply one of these methods to give the text a transformation:

➢ **Changing color:** choose the text, and on the Home tab, open the drop-down menu on the Font Color button and select a color. You can also click the Font group button to open the Font dialog box and select a color.

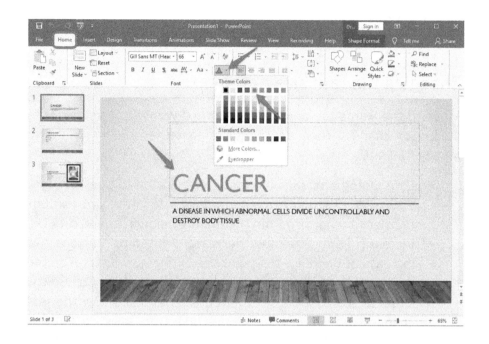

> **Selecting text fills, outlines, and effects:** select the Design tab, then click the Format Background button from the customize region. The Options tab in the Format Shape pane provides various ways to change the looks of text:

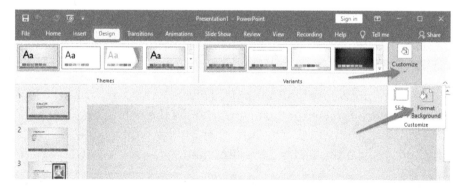

Then choose the text and click the Text Options tab in the Format Shape pane.

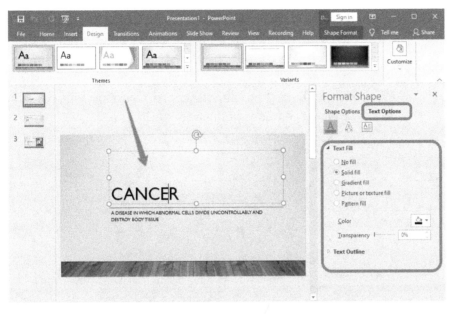

- **Fill:** Display the text in gradients, patterns, or textures. You can designate or select a transparent color for text by selecting a color and dragging the transparency slider, see the image above.
- **Outline:** Modify the text outline- the extreme lines that fashion the numbers and letters. Apply this: beneath Fill, select the No Fill option, and then select a solid line as the outline.

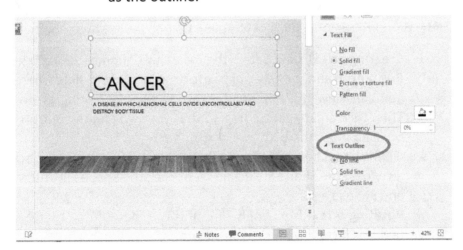

- **Effect:** Provide the numbers and letters a shadow, a glow, a reflection, a softer edge, or another aspect. Before you try-out these instructions, try selecting an option on the presets catalog. Preset options show what these text effects can do and provide you an advantage in designing a text effect.

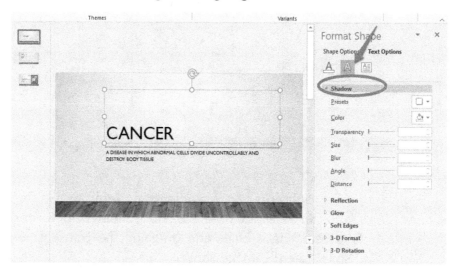

Thrill with Text Boxes and Text Box Shapes

Text boxes permit you to exercise your creativity. They include another element in the slides. Apply them to place text anywhere you wish, explain a chart or equation, or position an announcement on a slide. Here are the principles of handling text boxes in PowerPoint:

- ➤ **Creating a text box:** Select the insert tab, then click the Text Box button and shift the pointer to an aspect of the slide where you can view the box pointer, a downward-pointing arrow. Then click and begin to drag so that you can create your text box and input the text.
- ➤ **Filling a text box with color:** click the Shape Format tab, select a style on the Shape Style gallery, or click the Shape Fill button and choose a color.
- ➤ **Rotating a text box:** apply one of these methods to rotate a text box including the text inside it:

- Drag the rotation handle and the circle above the text box.
- On the Shape Format tab, click the rotate button and select a Flip or rotate command on the drop-down catalog.
- On the Format tab, click the size group button (you may have to select the Size button first) then in the Format Shape pane, insert a measurement in the rotation box.

➢ **Changing or modifying the direction of text:** On the Home tab, click the Text Direction button and select a Stacked or Rotate option.

➢ **Turning out a shape into a text box:** Build a shape, and then click on the shape and begin to type.

Guiding How Text Fits in Text Frames and Text Boxes

If the text does not fit in a text box or text placeholder frame, PowerPoint assigns to make it fit. In a text placeholder frame, PowerPoint contracts the amount of space between lines and then it contracts the text itself. If the text does not fit in a text box, PowerPoint extends the text box to fit more text. PowerPoint deals with overflow or flooding text as part of its Autofit mechanism. how AutoFit works is left to you. These pages describe how to select AutoFit options for flooding text in your text frames and text boxes.

Selecting how AutoFit works in text frames

PowerPoint has to AutoFit text when the text does not fit in a placeholder frame. The AutoFit Options button is displayed beside the text box. Click the AutoFit button to open a drop-down menu of options for dealing with flooding text. The AutoFit options-together with a couple of other methods, represent the "one at a time" way of dealing with flooding text.

Auto-fitting the text one frame at a time

Making the text fit usually means shrinking the text, extending the text frame, or compromising the slide design in some way. Here are diverse ways of dealing with the problem of text not fitting in a text frame. Be ready to click the Undo button when you try-out these methods:

- ➤ **Edit the text:** Normally the text needs editing when it does not fit in a frame. It needs to be made reduced. A slide is not a place for an essay or article. The only way to make the text fit in the frame without perplexing the design is by editing it.
- ➤ **Extend the frame:** click the AutoFit Options button and select Stop Fitting Text to this Placeholder on the shortcut catalog. Then choose the frame and drag the beneath or top selection handle to extend it.
- ➤ **Decrease the font size:** choose the text, move to the Home tab, and select a smaller Font Size measurement. You can also pick the Decrease Font Size button or (press Ctrl+<) to decline the font size.
- ➤ **Diminish the amount of spacing between lines:** select the Paragraph group button on the Home tab, to open the Paragraph dialog box and decline the After measurement under Spacing.
- ➤ **Change the frame's internal margins:** like a page, text frames have internal margins to protect the text from getting too close to a frame border. By declining these margins, you can create more room for text. Right-click the text frame and select Format Shape. Then, in the Format Shape pane, navigate to the Size & Properties tab, and beneath the Text Box settings insert smaller margin measurements.
- ➤ **Construct a new slide for the text:** if you are bargaining with a list or paragraph text in a body text frame, the AutoFit Option drop-down catalog provides ways to construct a new slide. Select continue on the New Slide to run the text onto another slide; select Split Text Between Two Slides to separate the text equally between two slides.

Selecting default AutoFit options for Text Frames

Except if you modify the default AutoFit options, PowerPoint compresses the amount of space among lines and then compresses the text itself to make the text fit in text placeholder frames. Follow the steps below in case you want to decide for yourself if PowerPoint auto-fits text in text frames:

1. **Open the AutoFormat as you insert tab in the AutoCorrect dialog box.**

   See the two ways to get there below:
   - Click the AutoFit Options button and select Control AutoCorrect Options on the drop-down catalog
   - On the File tab, select Option to open the PowerPoint Options dialog box. in the Proofing category, click the AutoCorrect Options button.
2. **Disapprove the AutoFit Title Text to placeholder check box to stop auto-fitting in title text placeholder frames.**
3. **Disapprove the AutoFit Body Text to Placeholder check box to stop auto-fitting in title text placeholder frames separated from title frames.**
4. **Click OK.**

Selecting how Autofits works in text boxes

PowerPoint provides three choices for dealing with overflow text in text boxes:

- ➢ **Resize shape to fit text:** extend the text to make the text box fit inside it.
- ➢ **Shrink text on Overflow:** Shrink the text to make it fit in the text box.
- ➢ **Do not Autofit:** doesn't fit the text box but lets text spill out.

Follow the steps below to inform PowerPoint how or if to fit text in text boxes:

1. **Choose the text box.**

2. **Right-click the text box and select Format Shape.**
   The format Shape task unlocks.

3. **Move to the Size & Properties tab.**

4. **Show the text box options.**

5. **Select an Autofit option:** Do not AutoFit, Resize Shape to Fit Text, or Shrink Text on Overflow.

Arranging Text in Frames and Text boxes

How text is arranged in text frames and text boxes is controlled by two sets of commands: The Align commands and the Align Text commands. You can find these commands on the Home tab. By selecting combinations of Align and Align Text commands, you can place text wherever you want it to be in a text frame or text box.

➢ **Align commands control horizontal alignments.** Select the Home tab, click the Align Right (press Ctrl+R), Align Left (press Ctrl+L), Center (press Ctrl+E), or Justify button (press Ctrl+J).

➢ **Align Text commands control vertical alignments.** Click the Home tab, select the Align Text button, and pick Top, Bottom, or Middle on the drop-down catalog, as displayed in the image below:

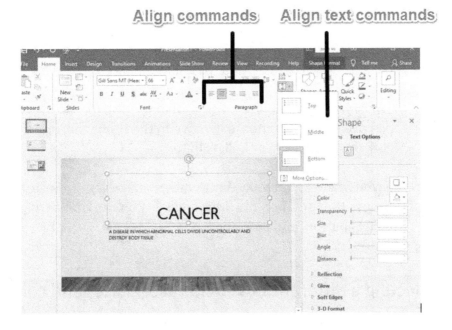

Dealing with Bulleted and Numbered Lists

PowerPoint without a list or two it's like a majesty without any clothes on, this aspect of the chapter describes all you need to know about bulleted and numbered lists. Lists It can be as easy and complicated as you want them to be. PowerPoint provides divers ways to format lists, but if you do not care if your lists look like everyone else's, you can take the opportunity of the Numbering and Bullets buttons and move with standard lists.

Making a standard bulleted or numbered list

Follow the steps below to make a standard bulleted or numbered list:

> **Making a bulleted list:** choose the list if you have already imputed the list items, select the Home tab, and click the Bullets button. You can also right-click, select Bullets on the shortcut list, and select a bullet character on the submenu if you don't worry about the standard, black, filled-in circle.

➢ **Making a numbered list:** choose the list in case you have inserted the list items, move to the Home tab, and click the Numbered button. You can also right-click, select Numbered on the shortcut list, and pick a numbered style on the submenu.

➢ **Transforming a numbered to a bulleted list (or vice versa):** pull over the list to choose it, move to the Home tab, and then click the numbering or bullets button.

if you want to remove the numbers or bullets from a list, choose the list, open the drop-down list on the Numbering or Bullets button, and pick None.

Selecting a different bullet character, size, and color

As the image below displays, the black filled- in circle is not the only character you can apply to mark items in a bulleted list. You can also select what PowerPoint regards as pictures or symbols from the Symbol dialog box. while in the process you can modify the bullets' size and color.

To apply pictures or symbols for bullets, begin by choosing your bulleted list, moving to the Home tab, and unlocking the drop-down list on the Bullets button. Use any of the bullets on the drop-down list or click the Bullets and Numbering option beneath the drop-down menu. See the Bulleted tab of the Bullets and Numbering dialog box, as displayed below:

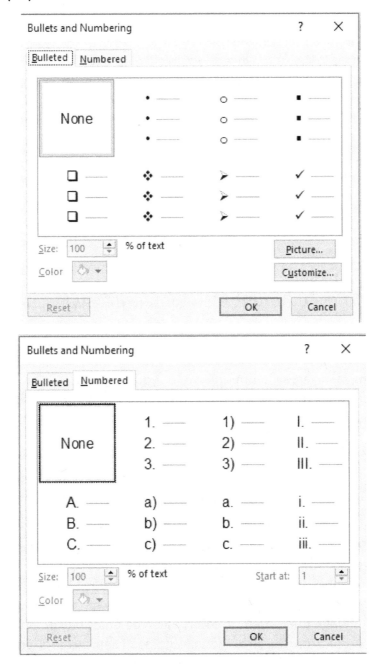

You can start customizing your bullets from the image above.

- ➢ **Apply a symbol for bullets:** Click the Customize button and choose a symbol in the Symbol dialog box.
- ➢ **Apply a picture for bullets:** Click the Picture button and look for a bullet in the Insert Pictures dialog box.
- ➢ **Change bullets' color:** select the Color button in the Bullets and Numbering dialog box and pick an option on the drop-down menu. Theme colors are assumed to most agree with the theme design you select for your presentation.
- ➢ **Change bullets' size:** impute a percentage figure in the Size % of the Text box. for instance, if you impute 200, the bullets are double as big as the font size you select for the items in your bulleted list.

Selecting a different list- numbering style, size, and color

PowerPoint provides seven diverse ways of numbering lists. Also selecting a diverse numbering style, you can modify the size of numbers comparable to the text and reform the color of numbers. To do these, start by choosing your list, move to the Home tab, and unlock the drop-down catalog on the Numbering button. Use any one you like from the numbering scheme options or click the Bullets and Numbering to unlock the Numbered tab of the Bullets and Numbering dialog box (see the image above). You can customize list numbers, from the dialog box.

- ➢ **Change the numbers' size:** insert a percentage number in the Size % of the Text box. for instance, if you insert 50, the numbers are half as large as the font size you pick for the items in your numbered list.
- ➢ **Change the numbers' color:** Click the Color button and select a color on the drop-down catalog. Theme colors are more agreeing with the theme design you select than the other colors.

Insert Footers and Headers on slides

A footer is a line of text that is displayed at the foot, or beneath, of a slide. A footer comprises the date, a company name, and a slide number, footer is displayed on every slide in a presentation. That does not mean you put footers on some slides or ban a footer from a slide, you can shift slide numbers, dates, and company names to the top of slides, and in so doing they become headers. This page describes everything you need to know about headers and footers- how to impute them, make them display on every or some slides, and ban them from slides.

Some background on headers and footers

PowerPoint offers the Headers & Footers command to insert the date, a word or two, and a slide number beneath all slides in your presentation. This command is the easiest way to insert a footer on the Slide Master without switching to the Slide Master view.

Inserting a standard footer on all your slides

A standard footer comprises the date, some text, and the page number. To insert a standard footer on all the slides in your presentation, click the Insert tab and select the Header & Footer button. See the Header and Footer dialog box, displayed below:

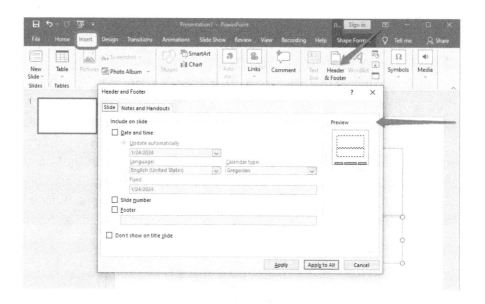

Select a few or all of these options and click Apply to All button:

> **Date and Time:** choose this check box to make the date display beneath the left corner of all your slides. Then inform PowerPoint if you want a current or fixed date.

  ▪ **Fixed:** choose this option button and impute a date in the text box. for instance, impute the date you constructed the presentation. With this option, the date stays fixed nowhere or when you deliver the presentation.

  ▪ **Update Automatically:** choose this option button to make the date and time display in the footer and unlock the drop-down menu to select a date format. With this choice, the date you deliver your presentation is always displayed on slides.

> **Slide Number:** choose this check box to make slide numbers display beneath the right corner of every slide.

> **Footer:** choose this check box, and in the text box, insert the words that you would like to display in the middle, or bottom of every slide.

> **Don't show on Title Slide:** Denials the footer from displaying on the title slide, most of the time the first slide in a presentation.

Constructing a nonstandard footer

To construct a nonstandard footer, follow these steps:

1. **Build a standard footer if you want your nonstandard footer to comprise the slide number or today's date.**
2. **Select the View tab, and then click the Slide Master button.**
3. **Choose the Slide Master, the topmost slide in the Slides pane.**
4. **Reform and format the footer text boxes to taste.**
5. **Click the Close Master View button to move from the Slide Master view.**

Removing a footer from a single slide

Removing one or all of the footer text frames from a slide is very easy, to do this, follow the steps below:

> Move to Normal view and show the slide with the footer that needs removing.
> Click the Insert tab and select the Headers & Footer button.
> From the Header and Footer dialog box that displays, disapprove check boxes- Date and Time, Slide Number, and Footer- to inform PowerPoint which aspects of the footer you want to remove.
> Click the Apply button.

> Be mindful not to click the Apply to All button. When you click this button the footers throughout your slide presentation will be removed.

CHAPTER FIVE

Making Your Presentations Friskier

This chapter aims to make your presentation stand out in a crowd. It provides ways to improve your presentation with charts, pictures, slides, and tables. It also displays how transitions and animations can make a presentation friskier. In conclusion, you will know how to play sound and video during a presentation.

Suggestions for Improving Your Presentation

Beginning from the Insert tab, you can do many things to make a presentation friskier. The Insert tab provides buttons for inserting tables, pictures, charts, diagrams, and shapes on slides:

Presenting Information in a Table

The motive of a table is to present information for juxtaposition purposes, a table is the best way to present a fast summary of the bare facts. PowerPoint provides not less than four ways to build a table. The best slide template for building tables is Title and Content because it provides space for a title and offers the Table icon, which you select to build a table. Build your table with one of these methods.

➤ **Drawing a table:** select the Insert tab, click the Table button, and select Draw Table on the drop-down catalog. The pointer turns into a pencil, use the pencil to draw the table borders. Select the Table Design tab, you can click the Draw Table button and draw the rows and columns for the table. Click the Eraser button to erase aspects of the table.

➤ **Using the Insert Table dialog box:** select the Insert tab, click the Table button, and select Insert Table on the drop-down catalog.

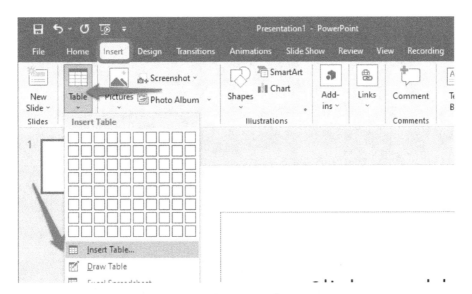

The Insert Table dialog box appears, see the image below.

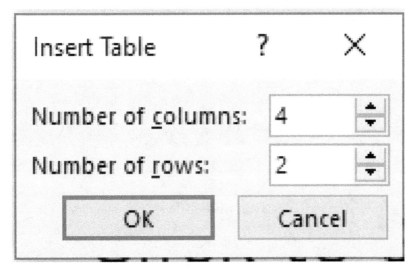

Then input the numbers of rows and columns you need and click OK.

> **Dragging on the Table list:** select the Insert tab, click the Table button, point on the drop-down menu to the number of rows and columns you need, and click, as displayed below.

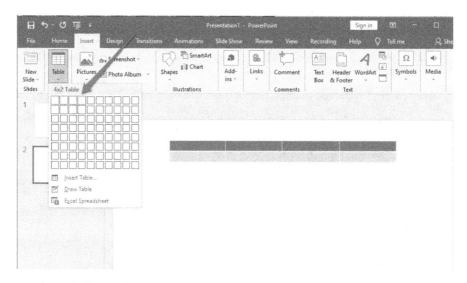

> **Clicking the Table icon:** select the Table icon in a content Placeholder frame. You notice the Insert Table dialog box, displayed below.

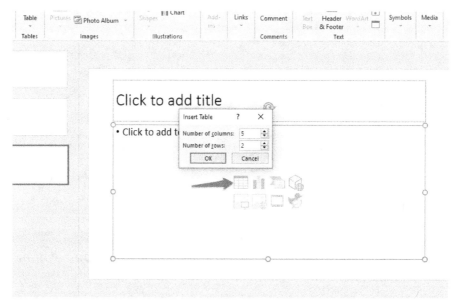

Digging through Transitions and Animations

A transition is a little bit of enthusiasm that occurs as one slide dematerializes from the screen and the next appears. An animation is a movement on the slide. For instance, you can animate bulleted lists in a way that the bullet points display on a slide one at a time when you click the mouse rather than all at a time. Transition comprises the Fade, Morph, and Push.

Putting transitions to slides

To display transitions between slides, choose the slide or slides that require transitions, move to the transition tab, and choose a transition in the Transition to This Slide gallery. If you want to apply the same transition to all the slides in a presentation, select the Apply to All button after you pick a transition.

The Transitions tab provides these tools for squeezing a transition:

> **Sound:** unlock the Sound drop-down menu and select a sound to escort the transition. The Loop Until Next Sound option beneath the drop-down menu plays a sound repeatedly until the next slide in the presentation displays.
> **Duration:** Insert a period in the duration box to proclaim how slowly or quickly you want the transition to happen.
> **Effect Options:** Click the Effect Options button and select an effect on the drop-down menu. For instance, select From the Top or Bottom to make a transition comes from the top or beneath the screen. Not all transitions provide effect options.

Changing and removing slide transitions

Pick a slide that requires a transition change, click the Transition tab, and follow these steps to change or remove the transition:

> **Changing a transition:** select a different transition in the Transition to This Slide gallery. You can also select different effect options and sounds and modify the duration of the transition.

➤ **Removing a transition:** select None in the Transition to This Slide gallery.

The animating aspect of a slide

You can select between animation schemes, the pre-built special effects created by elves of Microsoft, or your personal customized animations. Only those who are fans of animation and people with the luxury of time on their hands choose the second way.

Picking a pre-design animation scheme

Follow these instructions to preview and select an animation scheme for slides:

1. **Visit the Animation tab.**
2. **Choose the element on the slide that you want to animate:** for instance, choose a text frame with a bulleted list. You will know when you have chosen an element because a selection box encamps around it.
3. **Select an animation effect in the Animation Styles gallery.**
4. **Click the effect options button and examine with choices on the drop-down menu to squeeze your animation.**
5. **If you select a text-box or text-frame element with more than one paragraph in instruction 2, click the effect Options button and inform PowerPoint whether to animate all the text or animate each paragraph differently from the others.**

   ▪ **As One object or All at Once:** All the text is animated at the same period.
   ▪ **By Paragraph:** each paragraph is salted distinctly and it is animated on its own.

Very shortly, you will notice a preview of the animation choice you made. But to view a good look at the animation you just selected for your slide, click the Preview button on the Animations tab. Return to the Animation Styles gallery and select None if you want to remove an Animation.

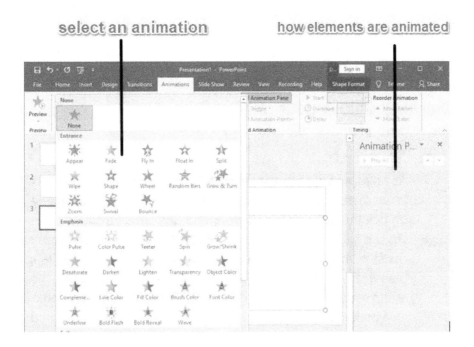

Designing your animation schemes

To design your personal animation schemes, visit the Animations tab and click to unlock the animation pane button as displayed in the image above. Choose an element on the slide and follow these steps to animate it:

➢ Click and Add Animation button and select an animation.
➢ From the start drop-down menu, affirm if the animation starts when you click your slide (On Click), at the same period as the previous animation (With Previous), or after the previous animation (After Previous).

- In the Duration box, insert how long you want the animation to stay.
- In the Delay box, impute a period to proclaim how soon after the previous animation in the Animation pane you would like your animation to happen.
- Choose an animation in the task pane and click a Re-Order button to reform the order in which the animation happen, if you animated more than one element on your slide.

Making Audio Aspect of Your Presentation

PowerPoint provides two ways to make the Audio aspect of a presentation:

- **As an aspect of slide transitions:** A sound is heard immediately after a new slide arrives onscreen. On the Transitions tab, unlock the Sound drop-down menu and select a sound.
- **On the slide itself:** the ways of Playing audio are displayed on the slide in the form of an Audio icon, as displayed in the image below. By shifting the mouse across this icon, you can show audio controls, and apply these controls to Play audio. You can also make audio play immediately after the slide comes on the screen.

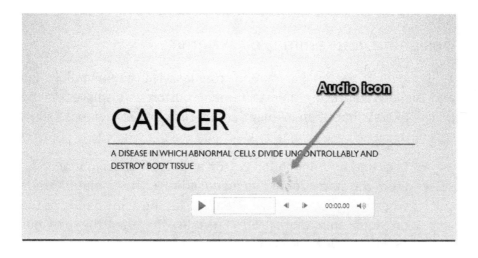

Inserting an audio file on a slide

Follow the steps below to insert an audio file in a slide:

1. **Click the Insert tab.**
2. **Select the Audio button**
3. **Select Audio on My PC.**
4. **Find and choose a sound file.**
5. **Click insert.**

To stop playing a sound file on a slide, choose its Audio icon and then press the Delete key.

Informing PowerPoint when and how to Play an audio file

To inform PowerPoint when and how to Play an Audio file, commence by choosing the Audio icon and navigating to the Playback tab, as displayed in the slide below:

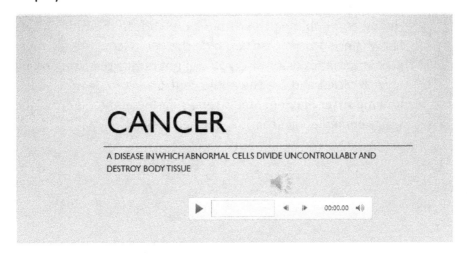

From here, you can control how and when audio files Play:

➢ **Controlling the volume:** Click the Volume button and select an option on the drop-down menu to control how loud the audio plays.

➢ **Playing the audio file automatically in the background:** Click the Play in Background button. You are telling PowerPoint to Play the audio automatically, all over slides when you click the button. Till you or another speaker stop the audio from Playing.

➢ **Deciding when and how to play audio:** click the No Style button. Choose the options below:

- **Play Across slides:** play the audio file across a presentation, not only when the slide with the audio file displays.
- **Loop Until Stopped:** Play the audio file continually till you or another speaker clicks the Pause button.
- **Start:** select Automatically to make the audio play immediately after the slide arrives. Select When Clicked On to Play Audio when you click the Audio icon on your slide.

➢ **Hiding and unhiding the Audio icon:** choose the Hide During Show check box. In case you hide the audio icon, the file must play automatically, or else you will not notice the icon and be able to click it and see the audio controls.

➢ **Rewind After Playing:** Starts replaying the audio file from the starts immediately after it is finished playing.

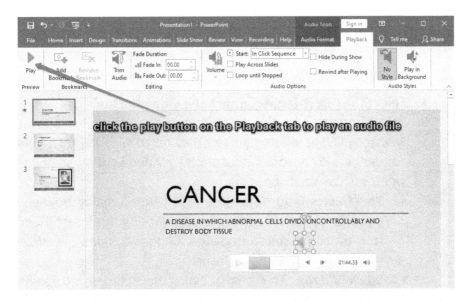

You can also click the Play button on the audio icon to play an audio file.

Playing audio during a presentation

Follow these steps to start, Pause, and control the volume of an audio recording during a presentation:

➢ **Starting an audio file:** Shift the Pointer across the Audio icon, and when you notice the Audio controls, click the Play or Pause button (or press Alt+P).

➢ **Pausing an audio file:** Click the Play/Pause button (or press Alt+P). select the button one more time to resume playing the audio file.

➢ **Controlling the volume:** shift the Pointer across the Mute/Unmute icon to show the volume slider and pull the volume control on the slider.

Playing Video on Slides

If you want your presentation to be more attractive you can play a video on slide. Follow the steps below to insert a video on a slide:

1. **Select the Insert tab, then click the video button.**
2. **Select an option on the drop-down menu.** There are diverse ways of playing video, you can play video files kept on your computer, play a stock video, or play a video kept on an online video such as YouTube.
   - **This Device:** you notice the Insert Video dialog box. you can also unlock this dialog box by clicking the Insert Video icon on some slide templates. Choose a video saved on your computer and click Insert.
   - **Stock Videos:** The Media dialog box comes into sight, move to the Videos tab, search for and choose a video, then click Insert.
   - **Online Video:** A dialog box for imputing video displays. Paste the URL of the video you want to display into the dialog box, then click Insert.

Modifying a Video Presentation

As displayed in the video below, choose the video and move to the Playback tab to modify a video presentation. The Playback tab provides many kinds of commands for making the video play to your taste. Visit the Playback tab to modify a video presentation

Here are the diverse ways to modify a video presentation:

❖ **Adding a bookmark:** Add a bookmark to be able to move forward or backward in the video when you play it. To add a bookmark, play the video to the position where you need the bookmark to be, then stop playing the video. The next thing to do is to click the Add Bookmark button. The bookmark displays in the form of a circle, click this circle to move to the bookmark while you play the video. If you want to remove a bookmark, choose it on the timeline and click the Remove Bookmark button.

❖ **Fading in and out:** impute time measurements in the Fade in and Fade Out text boxes to mark the video fade out or in.

❖ **Trimming the video:** To trim from the start or end of a video, select the Trim Video button. Then drag the green slider in the Trim video dialog box to trim from the start of the video; pull the red to trim from the end.

❖ **Controlling the volume:** select the volume button and pick Low, Medium, High, or Mute to control the loudness of the video.

❖ **Playing the video automatically or when you click the Play/Pause button:** unlock the Start drop-down menu and select Automatically or When Clicked On to inform PowerPoint when to start playing the video.

❖ **Playing the video at full screen:** To do this, select the Play Screen check box.

❖ **Hiding the video when it is not playing:** select the Hide While Not Playing check box. Be certain to select Automatically on the Start drop-down menu if you pick this check box.

❖ **Continuously Playing, or Looping, the video:** play the video continuously or till you move to the next slide by choosing the loop Until Stopped check box.

❖ **Rewinding the video when it is finished playing:** if you want to see the first frame, rewind the video when the video is finished playing.

Investigating the look of the video

if you want your video to look a little sharper, you are hereby invited to investigate with the commands on the Format tab and Format Video pane displayed in the image below.

To unlock the Format Video pane, move to the Format tab and apply one of the following:

➢ Select the Corrections button and pick Video Corrections Options on the drop-down menu.

➢ Select the Video Styles group button.

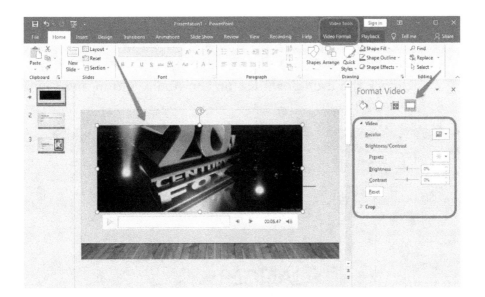

When you are in the process of investigating, choose your video and apply these methods for modifying its visibility:

> **Modify the brightness and contrast:** select the connections button and pick a setting in the gallery or modify the Brightness and contrast settings in the Format Video pane.
> **Recolor the video:** select the color button on the format tab, or the Recolor button in the Format Video pane, then choose a color or black-and-white option.

Recording a Voice Narration for Slides

the most appropriate way to record voice narrations is to do it on a slide-by-slide basis. You can record over many slides, but there can be many troubles getting your voice narration and slides to correspond exactly. Position your script before you and follow the steps below to record voice narration for a slide:

> **Pick the slide that requires voice narration.**

➤ **Click the Insert tab.**

➤ **Unlock the drop-down list on the Audio button and select Record Audio.**

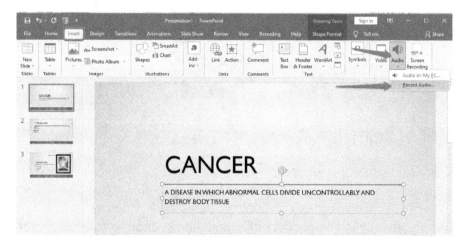

You notice the Record Sound dialog box displayed below:

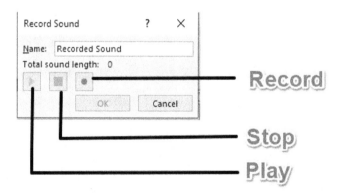

➤ **Select the Record button and start reading your script.** To pause the recording click the Stop button, to resume recording click the Record button, and to Playback whatever you have recorded so far, click the Play button.

➤ **Click the OK button in the Record Sound dialog box when you are done recording the narration for your slide.** The Audio icon displays on your slide that your slide is escorted by an audio file. Your next work is to choose the icon, move to the Playback tab, and inform PowerPoint when to play the audio recording, the volume range, and if you want it to loop.

CHAPTER SIX

Delivering a presentation

Now, we have come to where we have been anticipating, it is time to deliver the presentation. This chapter describes how to practice your presentation to discover how long it is and how to display your presentation. You will come across some methods to make your presentation friskier, how to draw on slides using a pen or highlighter and blank out the screen to gain the spectator's ultimate attention, and many more skills to give a wonderful presentation.

What you need to know about Notes

Notes are meant for the speaker. The audience cannot see them. Do not think twice or waver to write notes to yourself when putting together your presentation. The notes will appear conveniently when you are practicing and delivering your presentation. They provide you with a concept of what to say and assist you in communicating better. Here are the steps for entering, editing, and printing notes:

> **Entering a note:** To impute a note, begin from Normal or Outline view and impute the note in the Notes pane. If the Notes pane is not shown, click the Notes button on the view tab or status bar.

> **Editing notes in Notes Page view:** After you have penned down your notes, go to Notes Page view and edit them. To return to the Notes Page view, select the view tab and click the Notes Page button. Notes are displayed in a text frame beneath a picture of the slide they belong to. You may need to zoom in to read them.

> **Printing your notes:** click the File tab, and select Print. You notice the Print window. Below Settings, unlock the second drop-down list and select Notes Pages on the pop-out list. Then click the Print button.

Practicing with a Robot Coach

Unlock a presentation you have worked so hard to build and follow these instructions to see if PowerPoint's robot coach will be of help:

> **On the Slide Show tab, select the Rehearsing with Coach button.**
> **Click the Start Rehearsing button and deliver your Presentation.** Imagine you are delivering your presentation before a real spectator. Move from slide to slide, keeping the speed you expect to keep. As you move ahead, PowerPoint provides the word of encouragement in the box beneath the right corner of the screen.
> **Examine the rehearsal report and notice where PowerPoint says you can do better.**

Practicing and Timing Your Presentation

It is good to practice your presentation, the more you practice, the more convenient you are delivering a presentation, therefore make sure you rehearse your presentation over and over again. Follow these steps below to practice a presentation, record its duration, and record how long each slide is shown:

> **Choose the first slide in your presentation.**
> **Move to the Slide Show tab.**
> **Pick the Rehearse Timings button.** The Recording toolbar displays then you move to the Slide Show view.
> **Deliver your presentation one slide at a time and click the Next button on the Recording toolbar to navigate from slide to slide.** Immediately each slide displays, think as if you are presenting it to your audience. Say what you want to say during the real presentation. You can do so many things from the Recording toolbar provides you such as moving to the next slide by clicking the Next button, clicking the Pause Recording

to stop the recording for a moment when you want to attend to some other things then clicking Resume Recording button to continue recording, and also click the Repeat button in case you want to start over with a slide.

➢ **From the dialog box that asks if you want to keep the slide timings, note how long your presentation is**

➢ **In the dialog box that asks whether you want to keep the recent slide timings, select Yes if you want to how long each slide remains on the screen during the rehearsal.** Immediately after you click Yes, you can visit the Slide Sorter view and discover how long each slide stayed on the screen.

Showing Your Presentation

These pages will enlighten you on how to start and end a presentation, all the diverse ways to advance or retreat from slide to slide, and how to navigate to diverse slides.

Starting and ending a presentation

Here are the diverse ways to start a presentation from the beginning:

➢ On the Quick Access toolbar or Slide Show tab, click the From Beginning button.

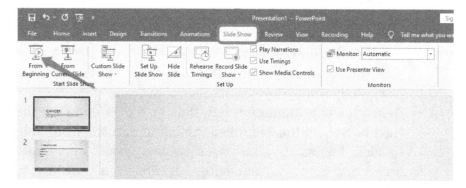

➢ Choose the first slide and click the Slide Show view button on the status bar.

You can begin a presentation in the middle by choosing a slide in the middle and then clicking the Slide Show view button.

Here are the diverse ways to end a presentation untimely or beforehand:

➢ Press Esc
➢ Click the Slide Control button and select End Show on the pop-out list. The Slide Control can be found beneath the left corner of the screen
➢ Right-click and select End Show in the shortcut list.

Moving from slide to slide

PowerPoint provides four ways to navigate or move from slide to slide in a presentation which is:

➢ **Click the Next or Previous button:** this button can be found below the left corner of the screen.
➢ **Right-click on the screen:** Right-click and select a navigation option at the top of the shortcut list.
➢ **Press a keyboard shortcut:** press one of the many keyboard shortcuts that PowerPoint provides for moving from slide to slide.
➢ **Click the Slides button and select a slide.**

Moving forward or backward from slide to slide

To move forward from slide to slide following slide in a presentation, click on the screen, immediately after you click, the next slide shows. If all goes well, clicking is the only method you need to know when delivering a presentation to move from slide to slide.

Jumping forward or backward to a particular slide

If you find it essential to jump forward or backward over many slides in your presentation to arrive at the slide you want to display, it can be done with these methods:

> ➢ Click the Slides button beneath the left corner of the screen. In thumbnail versions of the slides in the presentation display, click the thumbnail to see a slide.
> ➢ Press Ctrl+S. You will see the All dialog box. it outlines all slides in your presentation. Choose the slide you want to display and click the Go To button.

Tricks for Making Presentations a Little Joyous

Here are a few tricks to make your presentations a little joyous. I discuss how to draw on slides, highlight aspects of slides, blank the screen, and zoom in. Take these tricks and apply them to your next PowerPoint presentation to make it stand out.

Using a pen or highlighter in a presentation

Drawing on slides is a brilliant way to add a little joy to a presentation. Lash out a pen and draw on a slide to get the spectators' attention.

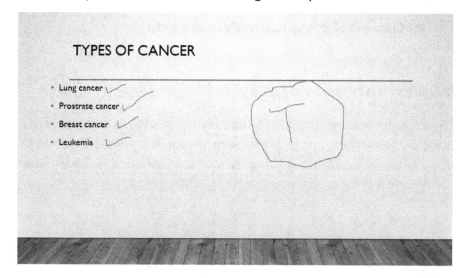

Drawing or highlighting on a slide

Follow these instructions during a presentation to draw or highlight on a slide:

➢ **Click the pen button and select a color on the pop-out list:** The pen button can be found beneath the left corner of the screen.
➢ **Click the pen button one more time and select pen to draw on the slide or highlight parts of the slide.**
➢ **Drag the mouse to draw or highlight on the slide.**
➢ **Press Esc when you are done using the pen or highlighter.**

Hiding, erasing pen and highlighter markings

Follow these steps to hide, and erase pen and highlighter markings during a slide presentation:

❖ **Temporarily displaying or hiding markings:** Right-click and select screen- Show/Hide ink.
❖ **Permanently erasing markings one at a time:** Click the pen button and select Eraser. The Eraser displays, and then click a line to erase it. Press Esc immediately after you are done using the eraser.
❖ **Permanently erase all the markings on a slide:** press E or click the pen button and select Erase All Ink on Slide.

Follow these steps to erase or hide pen and highlighter markings immediately after a presentation:

❖ **Erase the markings:** On the Review tab, unlock the drop-down menu on the Hide Ink button and select one of these options:
  • **Delete All Ink in This Presentation:** Erase markings you made on all the slides in your presentation.
  • **Delete All Ink on This Slide:** Erase markings you made on a slide you chose.

- **Hide the markings:** Select the Hide Ink button, on the Review tab.

Blanking the screen

Whenever you want the audience to focus more on you and not the PowerPoint, always make sure you blank the screen, when you apply this method you will get your audience to focus on you.

Follow these steps to blank out the screen during the presentation:

➤ **White screen:** Press W, the comma key, or right-click and select Screen-White Screen.
➤ **Black screen:** Press B, the period key, or right-click and select Screen-Black Screen.

To view a PowerPoint slide again, click on the screen or press any key on the keyboard.

Zooming in

Another way to add a little joy to a presentation is to zoom in on slides. To draw the spectator's attention to an aspect of a slide, you can do that by following these instructions:

➤ Click the Zoom button beneath the left corner of the screen.
➤ Navigate and click the aspect of a slide you want the spectator to focus on.
➤ Press Esc.

Delivering a Presentation When You Can't Be There Personally

Here I discuss five ways you can deliver your presentation when you are not there in person follow me diligently as I will be showing you the methods one after the other:

Providing handouts for your spectator

Handouts are printed slides that you distribute to the spectator, it can either be one, two, three, four, or nine per page. To inform PowerPoint how to create handouts, visit the View tab and select the Handout Master button, you can make your choice under the following items below on the Handout Master tab to make your handouts more attractive:

> **Slide Size:** Choose Standard or Widescreen.
> **Handout Orientation:** Choose Landscape or Portrait.
> **Slide-Per-Page:** Unlock the drop-down list and select how many slides are displayed on each page.
> **Header:** Choose the check box and insert a header in the text frame to make the header display at the top-left corner of all handout pages. The items for the header include the company name, your name, and the location of the seminar.
> **Footer:** Choose the Footer check box and insert a footer in the text frame beneath the left corner of the pages of the handout. The items for the footer are the same as the items for the headers.
> **Page Number:** Choose this check box in case you want page numbers to display on the handout pages.
> **Date:** Choose this check box in case you want the date you print the handout to display on the handout pages.
> **Background Styles:** Unlock the Background Styles drop-down menu and choose a color or gradient.

To print your handout, click the File tab and select Print or press Ctrl+P. the beneath settings, unlock the second drop-down list, and beneath the handout, select how many slides to print on each Page. Then click the Print button.

Building a self-running, Kiosk-style presentation

A self-running, Kiosk-style Presentation plays on its own voluntarily. You can send it to one of your colleagues to play it or Play it from a Kiosk. Slides display on the screen one after the other without your effort, immediately after the presentation is finished, it begins again from the first slide. PowerPoint provides two ways to demonstrate how long you want each slide to remain on the screen:

➢ **Entering the time durations, yourself:** Move to Slide Sorter view and click the Transitions tab. Then disapprove the On-Mouse Click check box and choose the After-check box, as displayed in the image below, then inform PowerPoint to keep all slides on the screen for the same period, or select a distinct time duration for each slide:

- **Each slide has a different time:** one after the other, choose each slide and impute a time duration in the After-text box.
- **All slides at the same time:** impute a time duration in the After-text box and select the Apply to All button.

➢ **Rehearsing the presentation:** Rehearse the Presentation and save the timings.

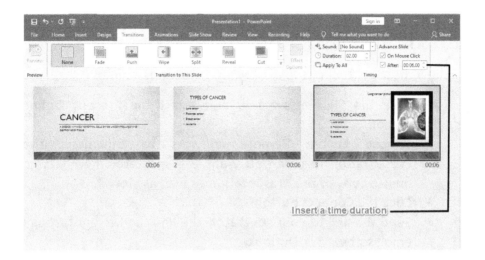

Informing PowerPoint that your presentation is self-running

You need to inform PowerPoint that your presentation is self-running before you can self-run, follow these steps below to make yours a Kiosk-style, self-running presentation:

1. **Visit the Slide Show tab.**
2. **Click the Set Up Slide Show button.** You will notice the Set Up Slide Show dialog box.
3. **Beneath Show Type, select the Browsed at a Kiosk (Full Screen) option.** When you choose this option, PowerPoint automatically picks the Loop Continuously Until 'Esc' check box.
4. **Click OK.**

Presenting a presentation online

Presenting online simply means playing a presentation on your computer for people who watch it on the Internet. As you move from slide to slide, spectator members view the slides on their web browsers. This is the best way to show a presentation to those who do not have PowerPoint.

Follow these instructions to display a presentation online:

- ➢ **Click the Slide Show tab, and select the Present Online button.**
- ➢ **Choose Enable Remote Viewers to Download the Presentation in case you want the spectator members to have a copy of the Presentation as well as view it.**
- ➢ **Click the Connect button.**
- ➢ **Send the link to your spectator:** the link can be sent through email software or Outlook.
- ➢ **Be certain that spectator members have received the email invitation and are set to view your presentation.**
- ➢ **Click the Start Presentation button.**
- ➢ **Then give the Presentation:** Apply the same methods to navigate from slide to slide as you apply in any Presentation. You will find yourself in the Present Online tab when the Presentation ends.
- ➢ **On the Present Online tab, select the End Online Presentation button; select End Online Presentation in the confirmation dialog box.**

Displaying a presentation as an animated GIF

This is another amazing way to display a presentation when you are not there personally, you can save your presentation as an animated GIF file. GIF (graphic interface format) is a series of graphic images showing one after the other. All you need is a web browser to watch an animated GIF.

Follow the steps below to save a presentation as an animated GIF:

- ➢ **Click the File tab and select Export.** The Export window unlocks.

- ➢ **Select Create an Animated GIF.** you will notice the Create an animated GIF window.
- ➢ **Unlock the first drop-down menu and select a file size**
- ➢ **Choose the Make Background Transparent check box in case you want to remove themes and backgrounds from slide images.**
- ➢ **Insert how many seconds you want each slide to appear.** Pardon my manners, all slides display for the same duration of time in the presentation.
- ➢ **If you want a few slides, not all slides, to display, enter slide numbers in the Slides text boxes.**
- ➢ **Click the Create GIF button.** The Save As dialog box unlocks.
- ➢ **Then select a folder for saving the animated GIF, insert a name, and then click the Save button.** Double-click the animated GIF file to unlock and play it in a photo application.

Constructing a presentation video

This is another amazing way to give a presentation when you are not there in person, record it in an MPEG-4 file and distribute the file to people. PowerPoint provides a command for constructing an MPEG-4 version of a presentation.

Follow the steps below to construct an MPEG-4 version of a PowerPoint presentation:

1. **Click the File tab, and select Export.**
2. **Select Create a Video.** The Create a Video window appears.
3. **Unlock the first drop-down list and select a display resolution for your video**
4. **Unlock the second drop-down menu and select whether to use recording timings and narrations.**
5. **Unlock the second drop-down menu and select Preview Timings and Narrations.**
6. **Click the Create Video button.** The Save As dialog box unlocks.
7. **Select a folder for saving the MPEG-4 file, input a name for the file, then click the Save button.**

CONCLUSION

I am so sure that you can now operate Microsoft PowerPoint after reading this mini-book, I believe you can now move around the ribbon tab, and also how to make a slide show that contains different effects, how to build a new presentation with the help of a template, how to insert clipart, charts, video, and sound to your slide, and how to add text, animation, and transitions to your slides, how to include borders, colors, and highlight to your presentation, and various ways to deliver your presentation.

INDEX